My
Arkansas,
My
Home

My Arkansas, My Home

An

Arkansan's

Rendition

in

Spoken

Word

Jason Irby

LOVE WITHIN LIFE

The author can be contacted at the following:
 Jason Irby
 501.907.6710
 jirby@aristotle.net

ISBN: 978-0-9846571-2-4

J-Starr Pro
P.O. Box 55883
Little Rock, AR 72215
j-starr@aristotle.net
lovewithinlife-jasonirby.com

Printed in the United States of America

This book is printed on archival-quality paper that meets requirements of
the American National Standard for Information Sciences, Permanence
of Paper, Printed Library Materials, ANSI Z39.48-1984.

Two Gentlemen

Many people ask me, why did you write this book? Well, this book consists of selected works from my *Love Within Life* series. This book came from the My Arkansas, My Home section within my book, *Love Within Life*. Why did I write this book? The answer is simple. It's because.

It's because of the unconditional love and support that I feel from my dad and my mom. It's because of family and friends. It's because of wanting to see my children grow and develop. When I speak of my children, I remember an occasion when I was swimming in the ocean for only the 2nd time in my life. While swimming, I found that I had accidently swam out too far (especially for an inexperienced swimmer). I remember thinking, "how am I going to get back?" My mind and my heart said, "I am not going to die today." Visions and memories flashed through my mind as I was there all alone. Then my body was compelled to swim toward a shore that I could not see. I would swim, but the waves would push me back. Out of some instinct, I began to follow the over under method. I swam over the waves that pushed me forward. I swam under the waves that attempted to push me backward. I continue to follow this method until I reached a point where I could see the shore and then to where I could stand upright. It's because, my faith in Jesus is my victory. It's because.

And now about the two gentlemen from which this dedication is entitled. I returned to continue my graduate studies at the University of Arkansas at Little Rock after laying out for about four years. It was during this second effort that I became acquainted with two gentlemen. The first gentleman was Bruce Plopper and the second was Dan Littlefield. Both are award winning professors. Bruce became my advisor, teacher and instructor. He navigated me through the last required hours of my graduate study. He would say to me and the class, "You are a scholar and you are the expert in your area of research." I guess some of us believed him. I went on to win awards for two consecutive years for research papers that I submitted into the KTA honor society's contest. The second gentleman, Dan Littlefield, is the founder of the Sequoyah Research Center on the campus of UALR. The Sequoyah Research Center is a one of a kind library and archival center. It hosts symposiums on contemporary Native American ideas, artistic and creative products, and culturally relevant issues that concern contemporary tribal people. Now, that is where this book gained its momentum. Bruce referred me to Dan and Dan introduced me to the inventory within the center concerning Native and African American History. I learned a lot about Native Americans, African Americans and America in general and the past 300 (plus) years of history. In researching their histories, I learned a lot about Arkansas. And as it is said, the rest is written in my books. This has truly been a journey and a great learning process. I thank you all. Tim, I'm saving the Tim and Sonnie story for "The Social Scene." Support the local libraries. They are more than reading and research centers. They have now also developed into community and comfort centers.

Table of Contents

My Arkansas My Home 1.3

A Lot Like Home
(Little Rock)

From wherever you live or travel,
those places you love to be or love to see.
Little Rock is like what you love. Little Rock is a lot like home.
Little Rock's east is a lot like Kansas,
flat with amber waves of grain,
Like Louisiana, wet where majestic and mysterious swamp trees grow.
Little Rock's south is filled with trees and forests like Washington of Seattle.
It has its share of hills where those beautiful pine trees grow. It has its
share of people horseback riding on large estates like Texas or Kentucky
Little Rock's west has big houses that hang off hills like Beverly.
The enthused climb a mountain called Pinnacle and view the gateway to
mountains called Ouachita. Sailboats break through waves on a lake
called Maumelle.
To the north, there are more hills and mountains. The hills lead to
Mountains. Mountains called the Ozarks. Homes rest in valleys, while
winter winds whistle through tall pines, oaks, and other hardwoods.
Downtown, the Rock's like no other twin cities.
The shore of the Arkansas River winds through the metro on both sides.
A city hall and a river trail occupies both sides of that ole river.
The metro is very likeable and loveable.
It's comfortable, quiet, yet the sounds of commerce fill the air
There is a Starbucks, McDonalds, Wal-Mart, or Wal-Green just around
the corner. Activities include the usual dining, shopping, museums,
theatre, and other arts and crafts. Other activities include fishing,
boating, swimming, hiking, climbing, biking, hunting, and so many
other sports and water sports.
Some streets and highways wind and dip and curve like a roller coaster.
      Some streets and highways wind and dip and curve like a roller coaster.
Some hilltops provide scenic views for miles around

Some days are as hot as a firecracker, and some nights as cold as ice
Little Rock is in the middle of everywhere.
Little Rock, from here you can get to anywhere.
Little Rock is like what you love.
Little Rock is a lot like home.
From flat to swamp like, from forest like and hills, to valleys and
mountains, and a river and streams, lakes and downtowns, metro and rural.

Arkansas Mines

Arkansas has Crystal mines in the Hot Springs and Ozark areas
Silver was mined in the North Little Rock area
Granite is mined in the Little Rock area
Many have found valuable diamonds in the Murfreesboro area
Oil and Natural Gas is still excavated in the El Dorado area
Natural gas has newly been discovered in the Fayetteville shale region
Arkansas has mines

Around America in Central Arkansas
(430, 440, 530, 630, I 40, and I 30 loop)

You can travel around America on the Central Arkansas loop. Let us
start at the I 440/I 530 interchange heading east. As you travel and look
over the guardrails you see an area like Cajun or gator country. The
water and trees are distinguished. Then at mile marker 6 you cross the
Arkansas river (south) on I 440 To the south the river looks like a small
lake stretching southward. To the north the river winds its way into the
beautiful skyline of the twin cities. As you approach the I 440/I 140
interchange look south and eastward toward the prairie land and delta.
The land of amber waves of grain, fish farming, and duck hunting. Rich
farmland where Arkansas produces food for your plate, where history
was made. For some this road is known as the gateway to the west. For
others, it was a trail where tears were left behind (Trail of Tears). Now
follow I 40 west, to the north you will see more wetlands, and then
those all important oil storage tanks come into view, the blood of
transportation. Driving westward you see the skyline southwestward and
the indications of rail-transit. To your north, the beginning of hills that
rise out of the earth where homes sit atop Highway 67 joins I 40 in this
area, 67 was once known as the great Southwest trail. As you approach
the I 40/I 30 interchange traveling west you view the downtown in the
distance. Skyscrapers, houses and buildings, hills and a skyline views that
is shared by twin cities. Then, as you cross the levy exit 152, you really
begin to witness the beauty of hills, valleys, and mountains in the
distance. The gateway to the Ouachita and Ozark mountains is now
revealed. As you approach the I 40/I 430 interchange you are still
reminded why Central Arkansas is a mirror of what is great and beautiful
about America. You remember why some areas are called "God's
Country." As you travel south on I 430 you cross the Arkansas River
(north) displaying the Central Arkansas river valley. When you look
north, Pinnacle Mountain looms in the distance, followed by rows and

rows of ridges leading to the Ouachitas and Ozarks. To the south of this point is the great "Big Dam Bridge" sitting atop the Murray lock and dam. Continue the I 430 drive across the river and up the hillside and view the scenic view of homes and businesses intermingled with tall pines and hills. As you pass the I 430/I 630 interchange, you cross one of the most traveled and newly developed byways in Central Arkansas Continue south and there are more beautiful Arkansas Palms (the Pine tree) beautifully aligned along the highway. About now you will approach the I 430/I 30 interchange. Motorist traveling from the great Mid-south and beyond, and traveling from the great Southwest and beyond all pass this point. Now head east on I 30, just like other areas across America, you notice commerce and transit at work. As you travel east, look across the pond to the south at mile marker 133, there is a mine where granite is extracted. That ridge behind the mine is called Granite mountain. Continue east until you reconnect with I 440. If you choose you can now travel north on I 30 into downtown until it connects with I 630. If you follow I 630 sites include the state capital, downtown, hospitals, malls, beautiful homes, businesses, the zoo, and many other city amenities. In the journey, the roll around the Rock you will have seen hills and mountains, rivers and ponds, forest and farmland, metro and wetlands. Within this loop, you will have traveled around America. Travel America on the Central Arkansas loop.

Little Rock
(a resort I call home)

I've written about that "scenic city"
I've written about "Central Arkansas"
I've written about "Arkansas mines"
I've written about "natural heights"
I've written about "a lot like home"
I've even written about "within one"
But enough still can't be written about how great and unique
Little Rock, the capital city of Arkansas is.
A resort I call home
Everything that I've seen anywhere else
I've seen a portion of right here in Central Arkansas
The businesses may not have the same name
But I can get the same varieties
We may not have an ocean
But we have miles of shoreline
The water ranges from caramel to clear, from bluish to turquoise
There are scenic views from mountaintops and valleys
There are hikes in the forest and dust on the farms
This place is like a hidden secret
And many don't want to let the secret get out
The weather is not extreme
The winter is not cold everyday
The summer is not really hot every night
Access to anywhere in the world is easy
We have historical locations and presidential parks
Little Rock is a resort in the middle of everywhere

Little Rock
(that scenic city)

We have high rises and high cliffs.
We have ranches and rivers.
We have farms and fields,
beautiful lakes and beautiful hills.
There is a mountain called Pinnacle and a valley called Napa
The natural state and its capital region
invites travelers to see a city of seasons.
Lights, Camera, Action
As we rock and roll, we walk and stroll
on jeweled streets of people whose hearts are gold.
From Clinton to Cantrell and Kanis to King, from JFK to McArthur
and Markham to Main and McCain, all are streets of the famous named.
From Reservoir to Roosevelt and Chenal to Kiehl
in between lies a river and an old mill.
Little Rock a city of interstates has interchanges,
North, south, east and west exchanges. The central Arkansas roadways,
I 430, I 440, I 530, I 630, 67/167, I 30, and I 40 are all great byways
that shows that scenic beauty and guides you around
that metro that leads to everywhere. Little Rock, that scenic city,
that gateway city of north and south, of east and west.
Little Rock is that scenic city of the diamond and natural state.

Little Rock
Central Arkansas

Where the Ozarks meet the Ouachitas, meet the River Valley,
meet the Timberlands, meet the Prairie, meet the Delta
Where the Mid-West meets the Southwest,
meets the Gulf-South, meets the Mid-South
Homes rest atop hills and mountains, sit along hillsides, riversides, and
mountainsides. Are nestled in valleys, in trees, and rise above the prairie
Where lakes range from crystal clear,
to turquoise, to blue, and to caramel brown
Where you can within an hour go from rock climbing, to trail blazing,
to water-ski, to four wheeling, to metro area activities
Where rivers and streams are perfect for recreation,
camping, boating, fishing, and other water sports fun
Where malls and markets, restaurants and flea markets,
stores and shops, dealerships and partnerships abound
We are artist, world champions, Presidential, world renowned,
we are impressive, reborn, revitalized. We are Mid-America.
We are Central Arkansas.
We are Little Rock.

Natural Heights
(Little Rock)

When I look at a map or travel across this great, big, and beautiful USA.
I've seen costal cities like New York, Chicago, Detroit, Miami, St.
Petersburg, Cleveland, and New Orleans. I've seen great plain cities like
Dallas, Oklahoma City, Charlotte, Minneapolis, Kansas City and
Shreveport. I've see mountainous cities like Denver, Los Angeles,
San Francisco, Atlanta, and Knoxville.
These cities have blocks of and some even have miles of skyscrapers.
Little Rock has a nice small city skyline of buildings,
but Little Rock is a city also surrounded by natural heights.
Little Rock is at the south gate of where the Ozarks meet the Ouachitas.
There are mountains like Granite, Chenal, Green, Pinnacle, and Walton.
There are valleys like Napa, Pleasant, and Caddo.
There are hills like Scenic, Park, Hanger, Crest, and Western. Then there
are the heights, oooh the heights. Forrest, Pulaski, Kavanaugh, Military,
and Cantrell are beautiful drives.
Little Rock has those-man made multi-story buildings.
Little Rock is a jewel, a precious jewel with city lights in the natural state
with those natural heights.

Skyscrapers on the prairie

As you ride along the highways and byways of
the Arkansas prairie land and delta,
you will see structures rising out of
the prairie land, out of the earth.
These structures tower toward the heavens
practically scraping the sky.
These structures are not huge trees
nor are they cell and television towers.
These structures are made of concrete and steel.
These huge buildings are seemingly in the middle of nowhere.
These structures even appear to be mystical
There structures are skyscrapers on the prairie.
As you approach the city of Stuttgart,
it is like approaching the emerald city
in the movie "Land of Oz."
Stuttgart is however called "Sugar Town."
Stuttgart is the world's leader in
grain production (particularly rice).
Other cities and townships on the prairie
have these skyscrapers but in
even a more rural setting.
These towns include Lonoke, DeWitt,
Gillett, Wheatley, Brinkley, and Helena.
These towns have skyscrapers on the prairie.
Most of these towns are located along highway 70
and I 40 in central, east, and southeast Arkansas.
These skyscrapers do not house people.
They are not floors and floors of offices.
The escalators do not transport people
wearing leather sole dress shoes or power suits.

These skyscrapers store billions of individual grain kernels
such as rice, beans, and corn.
The grain is stacked among each other,
story upon story awaiting transport to the world.
They are stored in these
Skyscrapers on the prairie.

Wabbaseka Heritage

I write, I walk, I run in the footsteps
and spirit of those who have gone before me.
Those men and women who have impacted
the state, the nation, and the world.
Those artist, authors, educators, and entertainers
Those doctors, lawyers, and engineers
Those policy makers, home makers, farmers, soldiers, and others
who work with their hands, their minds, their hearts.
Those legacy makers who have gone on before me
to create the Wabbaseka Heritage.
I art a child of that Wabbaseka Heritage
These legacies are quite an impressive group.
Born common folk but made immortal folk.
I write, I walk, I run in their spirit of the great
Willie K. Hocker
Eldridge Cleaver
Ernie Murry
Wabbaseka Vocal Aires
"And many others"
The children of Wabbaseka have spun the globe.
The produce of Wabbaseka has fed and clothed the world.
Wabbaseka is more than just a township.
It is a community. It is a region, an area.
Its territory spans from the scatters to the dump,
from the bayou meter to the county line, and
from where Flat Bayou intersects Wabbaseka Bayou.
Wabbaseka Bayou, that stream with a gentle current,
that Bayou of black clay (black clay bayou).
It spans the whole of the Wabbaseka School District.
Wabbaseka spans as far as spirits carry it.

Those who travel with that Wabbaseka spirit in their heart.
So much talent, so much skill, so great an impact
Those who bare the spirit of that Wabbaseka Heritage.
That is why I write. I walk. I run in the footsteps
and spirit of those who have gone before me.
Those who are children of that Wabbaseka Heritage.
Those who have made history
and those from which history will be made.
Wabbaseka, Wadittesha, Wattiska, Wabbaseekee, Water Seca,
Watersky, Wataseka Island, Wabbasesa, Wabba seka, or however the
pronunciation may be. The name interpreted as "gentle flowing stream."
We write. We walk and we run in the footsteps
and spirit of those who have gone before us.
We are the children of that Wabbaseka Heritage.

Wabbaseka
(my home town)

I wrote a song about growing up in a small town.
My childhood hometown, Wabbaseka Arkansas
which means "gentle flowing stream"
The emphasis was how I'd felt it helped me to
stay grounded and enjoy the beauty of many things.
The lyrics and words went something like this.
"I grew up in a small town, small school, small church,
and a corner store. Granddaddy had a farm, white house,
red barn, and chickens on the front lawn. I've never been
to jail before, enjoying freedom is all I know."
I once wrote some words about a small town person.
I felt this person could look north, south, east, and west
and could see endlessly without obstacles blocking
the vision. Maybe there was a tree in the distance,
but no tall building or skyscraper, cluster of high rises
stretching for blocks and blocks to impair the vision
or dream. I thought I could see endlessly to the ends of
the earth as the sky sloped over the land like a bowl.
During summer nights, I could hear the insects sing in
unison to form what sounded like nature's orchestra.
My home town was so great because it reached so far.
It fed and clothed the world. The people from there
had such a great impact on the state, the nation, the world.
I wrote about how great an impact the children of Wabbaseka
have made. The writing is simply called "Wabbaseka Heritage."

Within one
Little Rock

Within one hour
I can go to view a mountain range
Visit a marsh and grasslands
Float in lakes so beautiful
ATV play in the mud
Cross vibrant rivers
Toss stones across clear flowing streams
Within one hour
I can stand among tall timber
Embrace high cotton
Ahhhh at winding rice levees
Visit fish and hog farms
Roam horse and cattle ranches
Awake to the rooster's crow
Within one hour
I can drive winding hillside roads
Cruise the city streets
Shop the malls and stores
Do the restaurants and festivals
Enjoy concerts, theater, and museums
Gaze at the stars and city lights
Within one hour
I can, in Little Rock
I can, in Central Arkansas

Oooouu Arkansas

Arkansas is the natural state
Lots of hills, fields, trees, and don't forget the lakes
And the city, capitol city, is Little Rock
So anytime you're passing though, you'd better stop
Arkansas is the DIAMOND state
With big cars, super stars, and big bank
And the people, yes the people are just keeping it real
The only diamond state and the home of Bill
Arkansas is a wondrous land
Every person in the state and every man
The Ozarks, Ouachitas, and waterfalls
Razorbacks and Travelers let's play some ball
Now let's all remember Paul Ellis
The voice of the Hogs for so many years
He's up in Hog heaven looking down on us all
Saying "oh my, oh my Arkansas!!!"

We AR
{Arkansas}

We are the natural state
We are the great escape
We are, we put food on your plate
Arkansas, Arkansas
Arkansas grows diamonds, and Crystal Hills,
Little Rocks, Hot Springs, and Rice Fields
Melon patches, fruit orchards and garden foods
Southern cooks, duck hunters, and Delta Blues
We have hometowns like Maumelle
College town like Fayetteville
New school like Marion
Old school like Washington
Hard as a Little Rock
Soft as an Ash Down
Tough as a Fort Smith
Small as a Tiny Town
Arkansas is a little state standing tall
We're the Razorback state let's play some ball
Pretty lakes, waterfalls, and precious stones
Pinnacle, Petit Jean and log cabin homes
The flag town like Wabbaseka
The beautiful like Bella Vista
No other state has the diamond rock
Ozark, Ouachita, rock around the clock

My
Arkansas
My
Home

1.3

Across the way

When you look across the way I want you to see the beauty in your path
Many have traveled the same path, that same path
Many have finished victoriously. All have finished victorious
Some have returned to loved ones. Many have joined loved ones
As you travel the path, I want to provide beauty along the way
I want you to see beauty as you look across the way
Many who finish, returning to loved ones say, "The path is not easy."
Many say the path is painful, many say the path is very painful
But all who enter the path, they endure to the best of their ability
As the Bible says, they endure to the degree at which God has given them
But as you travel your path, I want you to see the beauty across the way
I want to provide you with beauty as you travel across the way
Now you stand as so many have stood before you in times past
You now stand at the threshold of the path that leads to your victory
Now that you stand in the mist of that path surrounded by history
Can you see beauty? Can you see the beauty across the way?
Can I provide you with beauty as you travel across the way?
I want you to see that there is beauty across the way

Granny
(My prize)

When I realized how special you are
When I realized how much you have impacted my life
When I realized how much you really mean to me
I realized that you are
My past, My present, My prize
Not everyone has the opportunity to meet their granny
Not everyone has the chance to be lovingly held by their granny
Not everyone can give that love back
I realized that you are
My past, My present, My prize
Your ways have tickled me and I laugh
Your wisdom has strengthened me and I stand
Your wrath has corrected me and I cry
I realized that you are
My past, My present, My prize
Your blood runs warm through my veins
Your love runs deep in my brains
You are food to my soul
I realized that you are
My past. My present, My prize
When I realized how special you are,
I noticed that time never stands still,
I noticed that good memories last forever
I realized that you are
My past, My present, My prize

Us in them

I've watched the Blue Angles fly
They swoop and glide with precision, skill, and grace
But I've seen that same precision, skill, and grace in a flock of birds.
The eagle, ducks, geese, sparrows existed long before the blue angels.
I've watched a man in a rowboat.
He gracefully moved and steered the craft through the water.
Then I've seen this little bug floating on the water.
His appearance resembled that rowboat, but the bug was first
I've seen man defend and protect with a submarine.
That powerful submarine streaked through the water.
I've seen that same power and grace when I see certain fish.
The shark, barracuda, the bass, were here before the missile.
Man thinks he invented the ultimate "celebration"
To watch a new year's "rocking" eve with confetti raining down
or to watch the ticker tape fall from high onto a parade.
Have you never watched the leaves fall from trees in autumn's wind?
There are many other examples of us in them.
The dragonfly is the helicopter.
Tall mountains with caves are skyscrapers.
The bat is a radar and a snake is heat and seek.

My first mother

My first mother was earth from which I came
From earth I came to earth I will return
Ashes to ashes and dust to dust

Have you ever?

Have you ever seen the sunrise,
not over the mountains
not over the tree tops or
the tall buildings
but over the grass and fields?
Have you ever seen a body of water,
not as blue as the sky
not as turquoise as a gem or
as clear as a crystal
but as brown as a soothing cup of hot chocolate?
Have you ever seen a flame of fire,
not blazing on a stovetop
not as a destroying force
or flickering on top of a candle
but warming your hands while you gather around a campfire?
Have you ever seen a baby deer,
not in a petting zoo
a rabbit not in a cartoon
or a raccoon not made into a hat in a visitors' center
but all living in harmony
in their nature's home?
Have you ever?
I have, in Arkansas.

Art is

Art is everything created, made, that is
Art is a way, an avenue to (beautifully) express those things that are
Art comes in many forms to express the many things that are
Some men will attempt to own art when they can't have what is
That form of art may be a painting, a sculpture, a song, a poem
These forms express for him what he can't express himself
Art makes available that "what is" about him
Poetry is a written form of art, the word
These words beautifully and gracefully express in writing
Things that are, that were, that will be, and those things that are hoped
These words are on paper, statues, earth, stone, wood, and in hearts
Poetry fills the mind and allows for the window of imagination to open
Poetry is skillful, technical, and even spiritual
Words travel, intertwine, embrace, and even disperses one's being
Music is a vibration that entertains and stimulates the mind and soul.
It causes one to move and be moved from within and out. Styles of
music stimulate and inspire individuals differently. Music is a skill. One
may strum or pick strings with the fingers. One may impart breath by
mouth. One may even tap the feet or flop and flail an instrument by
hand. Music is an imitation of sounds that are within one's own
atmosphere. They say that music is a universal language
because the vibe is familiar to all

Bridges

There are bridges that connect us all.
My teacher is your aunt, is my aunt's best friend.
Your boss is my best friend's cousin.
My enemy is your brother's wife's mother.
There are bridges that connect us all.
DNA has no boundaries, colors or creeds.
Many in foreign lands have the same blood lineage.
That DNA connects us all from around the world.
These are bridges that connect us all.
Friendships, relationships are among the many bridges.

ARkansas Children

There are   Hills   Mountains   and Valleys to climb
     Blue Hill, Mountain View, Caddo Valley
     Springhill, Mountain Home, Scott Valley
     Cherry Hill, Mountain Pine, Cherry valley
There are   Springs   Lakes   and Falls to refresh
     Eureka Springs, Lakeview, Falls Chapel
     Hot Springs, Lake Village, Fallen Creek
     Heber Springs, Lakewood, Cedar Falls
There are   Cities   Villages   and Towns to live
     Star City, Cherokee Village, Tiny Town
     Forrest City, Village Creek, New Town
     Arkansas City, Village Junction, Gerogetown
There are   Bluffs   Ports   and Fields to explore
     Pine Bluff, Newport, Redfield
     Red Bluff, All Port, Springfield
     White Bluff, Jackson Port, Deerfield
There are   Indian names   Unique names   Foreign names
     Pocahontas, Possum Grape, England
     Osceola, Smackover, Stuttgart
     Wabbaseka, Arkadelphia, Palestine

                And in your love there is Hope
                     For ARkansas children
                     For ARkansas heritage

Arkansas' Travelers

You have built, created, and forged
Some left for fame, some from desperation
Arkansas' Travelers, come back home
But if you can't come back home, send back some love
- Maya Angelou—Author, Writer, Actress (The Queen of Poetry)
- Bill Clinton—42nd President of the United States
- Glenn Campbell—Country Music Singer (The Rhinestone Cowboy)
- Al Bell—Music Industry (The Soul Man)

You have span the globe, the nations, hearts and minds
You've formed the Houston's, the Chicago's, the ATL's, LA's and D.C.'s
Arkansas' Travelers come back home
But if you can't come back home, send back some prosperity
- T J Holmes—International Journalist
- Billy Bob Thornton—Award winning Hollywood actor and producer
- Brooks Robinson—Baseball Hall of Famer
- Hillary Clinton—Former First Lady, US Secretary of State

You are so beautiful, so talented, so giving
Some left to chase a dream, some to taste a dream
Arkansas' Travelers come back home
But if you can't come back home, send back some hope
- Jerry Jones—NFL Owner of the Dallas Cowboys
- Derrick Fisher—NBA multiple Championships (NBA Players
    Union President)
- Mark Martin—NASCAR
- Scottie Pippen—NBA multiple Championships

You were endowed, imparted, inspired
That gift within you has empowered many and many more

Arkansas' Travelers come back home
But if you can't come back home, send back your blessing
- Tory Hunter—Baseball
- NeYo—Music, Entertainment Industry awards winner
- Amy Lee—Grammy Awarded musical performer
- Mike Huckabee—former Arkansas governor, talk show host

You have built, created, and forged
Some left for fame, some from desperation
Arkansas' Travelers, come back home
But if you can't come back home, send back your love

Granddaddy had a farm
(My childhood steps)

My granddaddy had a farm with a white house, red barn, and chickens on the front lawn, a Blue Tick Hound and an A model John Deere tractor. The house was far off the paved highway about a half of a mile or so. To get to the house you had to drive down a long dirt road. A mud road when it rained. The farm was surrounded by fields of grain or cotton. I never picked or chopped cotton as work, but only as play. I would run through the field gathering cotton to place in Mama's (grand mom's) cotton sack. As a young child weighing 50 pounds or so, I would ride and sleep on mama's cotton sack as she dragged it up and down the rows picking cotton. Granddaddy's farm had a garden to the east of the farmhouse (52 childhood steps). In this garden he raised peas, beans, corn, tomatoes, okra, potatoes and other garden favorites. Just to the right of the garden was where an orchard began and to the right of it was the farmhouse (60 childhood steps). There were apple, pecan, peach, pear, and plum trees in the orchard. Also to the east of the farmhouse, far in the distance was a tree line standing by a ditch bank. A trees stretched miles southward and then westward around the farmland. To the west of the house was a canal (35 childhood steps), it ran north to south along the dirt road which lead to granddaddy's farm and ran (25 childhood steps) parallel to the farmhouse traveling north to south along the canal. My older cousins would cross the dirt road and swim in the canal. I remember that sometimes the dirt on the road would be so deep we could bury our feet about four or five inches under the surface. We as children played many a day in the dirt. We threw dust into the air, on ourselves, on each other. We ran in the dust behind cars, trucks, and tractors as they passed. We played with red wagons, tire swings and toy tractors. The barn (120 childhood steps) was also east from the house. We crossed the orchard to get to the barn. The south end of the orchard and the barnyard were connected by a foot trail. That path also connected the farmhouse and the barn. On that path, but closer to the barnyard was a well (80 childhood steps). The well, or "pump" as we called it had the best tasting, coldest water that we as children ever thought we had for drinking. Both drinking and bathing water came from this manual hand operated well (pump). Other water to wash clothing and watering the animals was collected in barrels of rainwater which flowed from the top of the tin roofed farmhouse. Behind the farmhouse (60 childhood steps) was an outhouse, John or toilet. It was so much fun going to that old wooden outhouse. If we needed to "use it" at night, we used a "pee-pot" that would be emptied the next day. We would have so much fun on the farm. I had a wonderful childhood running through the fields, playing in the dust, eating the fruit, seeing the animals, and being with granddaddy and mama (grand mom). Now granddaddy no longer has a farm. It was so heartbreaking, that day I realize that granddaddy had retired and moved from the farm and into a township. No longer did granddaddy have the white house, red barn, chickens on the front lawn, a barking Blue Tick Hound or a (A model) John Deere tractor. And now I no longer have my granddaddy. My granddaddy passed away. The farm with the white house, red barn, chickens on the front lawn, a Blue Tick Hound and John Deere tractor that granddaddy had is now just a vacant field. It is now a field with grass, grain or cotton. What are my great memories? Granddaddy had a farm with a white house, red barn, chickens on the front lawn, a Blue Tick Hound and a John Deere tractor. My childhood steps, my granddaddy's farm, in Wabbaseka Arkansas.

Le Belle Petite Rock

With a mountain like Pinnacle
With a lake like Maumelle
With a river like The Arkansas
The Rock is beautiful
The Beautiful Little Rock

With a Road like Cantrell
With a Parkway like Chenal
With an avenue like Clinton
The Rock is beautiful
The Beautiful Little Rock

As you sit in the stream in The Saline (river)
As you watch the sun set over the Mill (Old)
As you journey along the River Trail
The Rock is beautiful
The Beautiful Little Rock

With hills and valleys everywhere
With C 130s buzzing the air
Beautiful people here and there
The Rock is beautiful
The Beautiful Little Rock

Little Rock (diverse terrain)

A special look
A special feel
A special place
All because of the diverse terrain

Prairies to the east
Forrest to the south
Hills to the north
Mountains to the west

Diverse history
Civil war
Gang war
Family feuds

 National celebrities
Shooting stars
Open fields
All because of the diverse terrain

Soulman

From Central Arkansas, from North Little Rock, from the campus of
  Scipio Jones

From the Arkansas Delta, from KOKY studios, from the campus of
  Philander Smith College.

There came a man, a soulman. Songwriter, record producer, executive
  and now legend.

Born in Brinkley as Alvertis Isbell, his mother's baby boy, bundle of joy.

Known to us as Al Bell, the 6 feet 4, 212 pound prolific, music lovers
  pride and joy

To D. C., and Detroit. To Memphis and the Mid-South. To LA and all
  over the world.

This soulman, Al Bell has taken us there through the Staple Singers (I'll
  take you there).

This soulman, Al Bell has shown us where it is with the Tag Team
  (Whoop There It Is).

This soulman, Al Bell has marinated us in Soul, Hot Buttered Soul,
  Wattstaxx and Sweet Sweetback's

Al Bell is Hyperbolicsyllabicsesquedalymistic. Just ask Mr. Stewart, ask
  Mr. Gordy, ask Prince.

Al Bell, the lifetime Achiever. The women's pet, the men's threat, the
  play boys pride and joy.

Koky, Stax Records, Motown, Bellmark, ALBellPresents.

His body of work is developed, foundational, viable.

His face is accomplished, handsome, and prophetic.

His name is legendary, artistic, and regal

Even as the legacy continues, the Soulman launched his soul into
  cyberspace (the web).

His productions span from the "Rock" (Little Rock), unto the world
  and now into the heavens.

Son of the Arkansas Delta and Son of Central Arkansas

Child of North Little Rock and the campus of Scipio Jones
This Soulman, Al Bell is, The Soulman international, global and beyond
Al Bell is the Soulman

The Clinton

Located on the beautiful south shore of the Arkansas River, 42 steps east
   of downtown Little Rock,
4.2 minutes west of the airport and panoramically viewing the regions of
   the Natural State
The Clinton Presidential Center and Park (simply called "The Clinton"
   by locals) is truly a bridge
The Clinton is truly a bridge, a structure an institute, to help people
   cross, connect and communicate.
It looks like a sky bridge, a sky cap, a skyscraper that lays on its side,
   transparent, strong, stunning
A skyscraper that lays gently on its side so that many have the
   opportunity reach its top.
It connects service people to civilians. It connects politicians to the public.
It connects generations to generations. Generations once parted now
   merge, mix and mingle
It bridges communities to their country. Visitors enjoy concerts, lectures,
   and recreation.
The Clinton host local and international festivals, seminars, celebrations,
The Clinton is truly a bridge, a connector, a transport, a facilitator, a
   facility
The Clinton is interactive, beautiful, loving and alive. Discover the
   future, discover the past
Discover The Clinton

Wabbaseka Everything

A small rural town consisting of just fewer than 700 people when I
  lived there.
A city limit that spanned from the Wabbaseka Bayou to the Pecan orchard
My home town, Wabbaseka Arkansas was a city of everything. Earth,
  wind and home

Just like Sesame Street, the people that worked in the community were
  your neighbors
From shop keepers, farmers, and teachers to mechanics, plumbers, and
  preachers
My home town, Wabbaseka Arkansas was a city of everything. Family,
  Folks and Friends

Imagine a city so small having 3 or more full service stations. Gas, tires,
  oil installations
Several cafes, grocery/clothing stores, a bank, electronic repair men,
  laundry and car washes
The lawn services, the garbage men, the recycle men and Favors Dairy
  Bar shushes

Imagine a town so small, but we always had something to do
From basket, soft, base, soccer, dodge, kick and football to every other
  kind of ball played.
Wabbaseka was everything and I thought we had it all. Gardens,
  orchards and farms

Store hopping for candy and running to the cafe seeking the coldest
  drinks
Walking barefoot as thought we were in the sand but treading through
  the grass and dirt

Riding bicycles and ponies in open fields or alley ways and falling to
	the earth

Wabbaseka was everything and Wabbaseka had everything. Sunshine,
	rain and moonlight
No swimming pools but reservoirs. No ocean liners but farm tractors
And the people, yes the people, so culturally rich. Everything was
	Wabbaseka, everything

Ms Willie Was Watching

February 26th, May 24th through 26th, and July 27th 2013 were all dates when Alumni of Wabbaseka and friends gathered to pay tribute, meet and greet, remember the past and pursue the future. One hundred years have now passed since Ms. Willie's designed version of the Arkansas State Flag became the officially adopted flag of Arkansas. On February 26, 2013, Wabbaseka held the 100th year commemoration ceremony honoring the USS Arkansas, Ms. Willie's designed Arkansas Flag and Ms. Willie. And, Ms. Willie was watching. May 24th through May 26th, Wabbaseka School's alumni held an all school reunion. And, Ms. Willie was watching. Alumni from Willie K. Hocker gathered together at a citizen's home in Wabbaseka, July 27, 2013. And, Ms Willie was watching. Yes, Ms. Willie is watching her beloved Wabbaseka home from where it is drawn on a mural in Pine Bluff adjacent to the Jefferson County Court House and Martha Mitchell Highway. She looks northward across Lake Saracen, across the Arkansas River, across the Wabbaseka Bayou to her beloved Wabbaseka home. And now as Ms. Willie watches, the whole state will be watching, maybe even the whole country, maybe even the whole world. Ms. Willie will be watching as her officially adopted flag, the USS Arkansas, and yes Ms. Willie, will be deservingly honored by many, as her beloved hometown, Wabbaseka, erects the Arkansas Flag Memorial, Wabbaseka Memorial. Ms. Willie will be watching. October 12, 2013 and from this year forward, Ms. Willie will be proudly watching. Also from her beloved Wabbaseka hometown, Ms. Willie will be watching.

CPSIA information can be obtained at www.ICGtesting.com
Printed in the USA
LVOW01s0858061013

355618LV00001B/51/P

9 780984 657124